History for Beginners

Kallis Phoebe!

Mitte, et sa oleksid "Beginner", aga et "ajalugu" võtta teisest vaatevinklist.

Asta

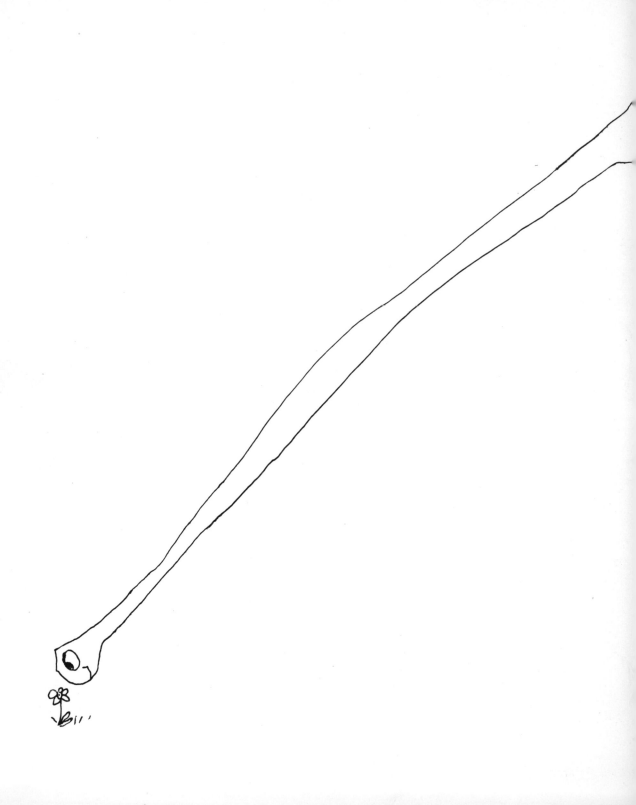

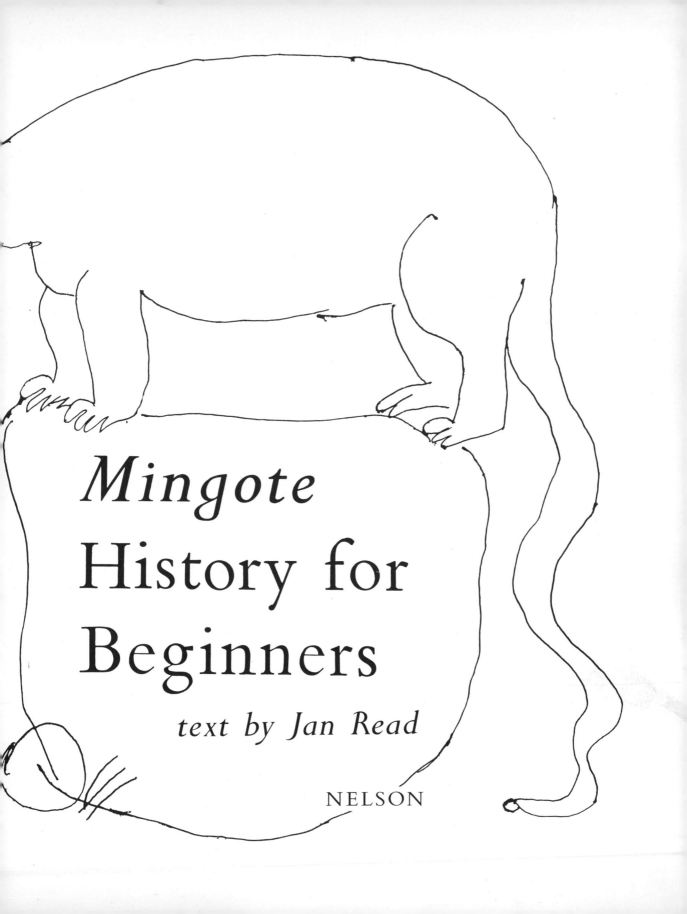

Mingote
History for Beginners

text by Jan Read

NELSON

THOMAS NELSON AND SONS LTD
Parkside Works Edinburgh 9
36 Park Street London W1
312 Flinders Street Melbourne C1

302–304 Barclays Bank Building
Commissioner and Kruis Streets
Johannesburg

THOMAS NELSON AND SONS (CANADA) LTD
91–93 Wellington Street West   Toronto 1

THOMAS NELSON AND SONS
19 East 47th Street New York 17

SOCIÉTÉ FRANÇAISE D'ÉDITIONS NELSON
97 rue Monge Paris 5

———

Printed in Great Britain by Thomas Nelson and Sons Ltd, Edinburgh

Preface

ARLY on the morning of 12 December, 1957 there were queues outside the massive portico of the Supreme Court in Madrid. The case had been reported in the London *Times*; and Moscow Radio had informed its listeners that a sense of humour was on trial in Spain. To the *Madrileños* the issue was more personal, for the intended victim was none other than their beloved Mingote, that shy 20th Century Don Quixote, who with pen instead of lance attacks the modern windmills of intolerance in the morning *ABC*.

The cartoonist's lot is not easy in a country where every drawing must pass the scrutiny of the Censor; but it was not the Spanish Government that was demanding for him a fine of 1,000,000 pesetas, four years' imprisonment and two months' banishment. Mingote, always alive to social abuses, had written an article satirizing the black market then rampant in the grocery shops, and his antagonists were the Guild of Retail Grocers. The drawing that appears overleaf did more than any defending counsel to win him an acquittal fêted throughout Madrid.

It is perhaps fitting that the man who so courageously upheld his legitimate right of criticism was a soldier until the age of twenty-seven. Always vividly interested in drawing, Angel Antonio Mingote traces the beginning of his professional career to jealousy of a gifted fellow student at college. No sooner was he satisfied that he could do as well, than his rival retired from the artistic scene to run a cork factory. Mingote, with a stack of drawings on his hands, sent them to the humorous review *La Cordoniz*. That was in 1945, and he has since contributed regularly to many Spanish periodicals, including *ABC*, *Semana* and *Don José*. He has also designed the decor for musical revues and films.

History for Beginners originally appeared as weekly instalments in *Semana*. Mingote had long been interested in history and costume; but the idea of preparing a humorous commentary on world history from the Stone Age to the present day dismayed even his bold spirit. He writes in the preface to the

Spanish edition: 'When Manuel Halcón of *Semana* asked me to undertake *Historia de la Gente*, I never thought that I would get further than the Phoenicians. However, man is a glutton for punishment. . . . I tremble to think of my plight, had I been born in the year 3847. . . .'

The present book contains a representative selection of drawings from the much longer Spanish version. The commentary is the result of collaboration with a writer who takes this opportunity of saluting his Spanish confrère and of stating that this is a text fulfilling no school or college requirement, or, in fact, any long-felt need whatsoever.

JAN READ

Contents

IN THE BEGINNING

The Stone Age

What little we know of Primitive Man we owe to the archaeologists and their excavations. It is certain that he was very much at the mercy of the weather; and in England, at any rate, then as now, the lower-lying ground was permanently swamped. Yet another hazard was the ever encroaching ice.

Thus it is that the Stone Age is divided into warm and cold periods. Whereas Early Paleolithic man hunted the elephant, rhinoceros, and hippopotamus, Neanderthal man lived amongst a cold fauna which included the mammoth, horse, ox, and reindeer.

When the weather was too bad to hunt anything at all our ancestors would while away the prehistoric days, fashioning rude pots or depicting scenes from the chase. This was a time when drawing on the walls was not considered bad manners.

The discovery of fire marked a turning-point in history, for fire made possible cookery, establishing once and for all the ascendancy of Woman over her weaker partner.

Obsessed as he was by a hard and intractable material, Stone-Age man was not an inventive fellow. Aeons passed before he put a handle to his stone; and at the end of a long day's hunting, dragging his spoils behind him, he was well pleased to retreat to his low-roofed cave and seek rest on his rocky couch.

Nevertheless, he has left primitive monuments in the shape of dolmens which allow us to reconstruct his emergence from below ground. Sometimes described as burial chambers, they combine shelter from the rain with a feeling for air and light. Modern Architecture owes much to them.

Sooner or later it was realized that two hunters can kill a dinosaur more easily than one. When they did without the dinosaur and gave themselves up to the simple pleasure of striking one another, history proper may be said to have begun.

The Bronze Age

The smelting of metals, first practised in Hither Asia, revolutionized habits the world over. Gone was the day of the plano-convex flint knife or the imported stone battle-axe from Scandinavia. Down the trade routes of that forgotten age, together with the bronze ornaments and needles, the plough-shares and the pots, travelled the first sword.

It was a rough weapon, handled with difficulty, which allowed a man to kill his neighbours one by one and face to face. It will readily be appreciated how long was the road that Man had yet to travel to reach his present state of perfection.

With changing materials came a change in manners. The primitive method of courtship was abandoned. It was found that only too often a blow from a cudgel affected a girl's head.

When it was the Other Man who took to providing such luxuries, the injured husband now had a potent remedy in his hands.

And women grew tired of the magnificent and comfortable furs, previously so fashionable, demanding instead trinkets and coarsely-woven, sack-like dresses.

A PARCEL FOR OSIRIS

Egypt

One of the first great ancient civilizations was that of the Egyptians in the Nile Valley. They were builders and sculptors on a massive scale ; the Pyramids and the Pharos at Alexandria ranked among the Seven Wonders of the ancient World.

IT SAYS 'FRAGILE WITH CARE' !

To an Egyptian the main purpose of this life was the preparation for his journey into the next. Were not the Pyramids, with their funeral chambers, veritable staircases to the sky ? Amidst all the thoughtful provisions for the trip, the most important thing in an Egyptian's baggage remains the Egyptian. They go down to history as innovators of the Mortician's Parlor.

Mesopotamia

Mesopotamia is sometimes called the cradle of western civilization. Here flourished the Syrians, Assyrians, Persians, and others. The Persians were distinguished for their skill with the bow and arrows, and they were also devoted to riding and fire-worship. To ancient Crete, with its Maze and Minotaur, must go the palm for the invention of bull-fighting.

Great sailors and traders, the Phoenicians were nothing if not business-like and habitually gave receipts. Realising the danger that their customers might understand the pictographs currently in use, they invented an alphabet.

Thanks to the clay tablets that survive them, our knowledge of the Babylonians is extensive. Their favourite pursuit was gardening, which they cultivated to such an extent as to lay themselves open to their warlike neighbours, the Assyrians, who spent half the time committing atrocities, and the other half writing commemorative inscriptions. Centuries later there were other peoples who enjoyed committing atrocities, but being more civilized they left it to their enemies to write about them.

ATHENS

Greece

Athens, mountain-built with peaceful citadel ; brown sails on a wine-dark sea ; Socrates arguing in the market place about the good and the beautiful ; the squaring of the circle and the golden mean ; a statue with a straight Grecian nose, so perfect that its sculptor fell in love and Aphrodite brought it to life—such was the Golden Age of Greece.

As Shane Leslie has it : ' One little people living under the Balkans had laid all the principles and precedents of Art and Literature, Architecture and Philosophy: In Plato, Mysticism took birth, and in Aristotle, Science. Two thousand years of modern progress could only add Finance and Journalism to the Athenian pediment ! '

Athens was not the only city of Greece ; near by lay Sparta, now friend, now foe. If Athens brought the peaceful arts to their peak, it is the Spartans who will forever mirror the military virtues. Even in war the Greeks were poetic, in defeat supreme. Down the long centuries the names of Leonidas and his handful at Thermopylae and of Themistocles at Salamis are as wine in the nostrils.

Even the sweetly reasonable Greeks were swayed by physical passions ; and the most famous war of all, fought over the unfaithfulness of the fair Helen, inspired the Trojan Horse and the emergence of the first Commandos.

The Greeks consorted freely with their Gods—often with surprising consequences. A siren would stop at nothing to get her man ; and faced with a choice, the Grecian maid was broad-minded to a degree.

Founders of the Theatre as we know it, the Greeks transformed
the earlier religious rites into flesh-and-blood drama. Great
dramatists such as Aeschylus and Sophocles used the tragic stage
'to purify the passions of fear and pity through the exercise of
them '.

Greek comedy never touched the same heights and declined
into a parody of urban manners, thus setting a pattern for the
West End and Broadway. The Greeks soon discovered that
the live stage is always in a state of crisis. For this reason the
expenses of production were borne by a chosen citizen, the
' choregus', nowadays referred to as an 'angel'.

Rome

The history of Rome is one of war and conquest. Reaching out from Italy, the city state first overcame the Carthaginians, thus making herself mistress of the Mediterranean, and subsequently pressed back the borders of empire to Africa, Asia Minor, Spain, and Britain.

Wherever they went the Romans brought law and order, and more lasting assets in the form of roads and aqueducts. The security of the Roman Empire depended upon its legions, which were governed by the strictest discipline. Mutinies were quelled by putting to death each tenth man in a row, a method which effectively stifled complaints.

As communications were stretched to breaking-point, it became impossible to grant home leave. The soldiers had to content themselves with what the country offered. And what sorts of entertainment could the village maids provide for the legionaries? Very few—so few that we can say there was only one. Thus it was that the Romans conquered, but were themselves assimilated.

AQUÆDUCTUS ROMANUS

In architecture and the arts the Romans borrowed largely from the Greeks. They simplified the drama by arranging for the actors to wear masks. This enabled the audience to tell whether a play was a tragic masterpiece, or merely funny, with- out waiting for the critics.

THE TRIBUNE

As every schoolboy knows, Caesar divided all Gaul into three parts. The Romans had previously divided themselves into three classes : the patricians, the plebs, and the slaves. Naturally enough the slaves had no rights ; but to protect the plebs, or common people, against their betters, the Twelve Tables of Roman Law were drawn up. Extended under the Republic, but ignored by the later Emperors, they form the symbolic basis for the legal systems of modern Europe.

THE LAWYER

ROMAN WAITING FOR HIS WIFE
(LATE) TO GO TO THE THEATRE

Among the main distractions of Rome in her decadence were the chariot races and gladiatorial displays. Though hardly on the scale later to be mounted in Hollywood, these were spectacular enough and definitely more exciting than their modern counterparts : motor racing and bull-fighting.

Gladiatorial fights began with the honouring of heroes who had died in battle by sacrificing the lives of their captives. The practical Romans soon discovered that the spectacle became vastly more entertaining if the captives killed each other ; still later they introduced a pleasing diversity into the opposition.

As regards racing, the Romans understood that to arrive first merely demonstrates a capacity for going fast, a quality much to be appreciated in a fireman, but lacking the drawing power of a healthy smash.

BARBARIANS OBSERVING THE DECADENCE OF ROME

The Coming of the Barbarians

The term 'barbarian' was applied in ancient times to a person who did not speak one's own language. The word is probably onomatopoeic, since to the cultured Greek, it represented a babble, as do foreign tongues to the Anglo-Saxon of today.

Chief of the barbarians were the Ostrogoths, Visigoths, Huns, and Vandals, fierce tribes from the northern boundaries of the Empire, who wandered from place to place without thought of founding a city.

Sapped as they were by the amenities of civilization, by bread and circuses, baths, and Falernian wine, the Romans were to suffer a rude awakening. Their indignation can be imagined when they realized that it was no longer the gladiators who were to be put to the sword, but themselves.

29

Efforts to assimilate the warlike Goths met with some success; but caught without his toga the Roman made a sorry figure.

THE HUNS
WHAT TYPES!

The reprieve was short-lived ; and the Romans faced an orgy of destruction. At the head of a victorious horde, Attila swept across Europe, from Constantinople to the Rhine. Checked after a terrible battle in Gaul, he reorganized his forces and marched to the walls of Rome itself. The city was saved at huge expense ; but the Empire lay in ruins.

The Huns themselves did not long survive their bloody defeat in Gaul, but retired discomfited to their ancestral halls, to drown their sorrows in wassail and carousing.

THE FIRST SUMMER VISITORS

The Vikings

The most northern of the barbarian invaders were the Vikings, known also as Norsemen, and in England as ' Danes '. Emerging yearly from the picturesque, if confined, Norwegian fjords, and garbed for Wagnerian opera, they sailed south in search of plunder. The sight of their long black ships spread terror along the coasts and inlets of half a continent.

So effective were their forays in England that at one time they controlled most of the country and were bought off only by a levy known as Danegeld, which in scope and rapacity came near to equalling our present-day Income Tax.

Some of the Vikings settled in France, where they became known as Normans. If formerly they were holiday-makers who plundered the natives, their descendants are natives who have established hotels and cafés to plunder the holiday-makers.

VALKYRIE INVITES A
WARRIOR TO ACCOMPANY HER

Dally as they might with the local
populace, the destination of all true
Vikings was Valhalla, the hall of
the slain, where Odin received the
spirits of dead heroes. Thither
they were borne from the field
of battle and through the lowering
storm by the Valkyries, strapping
maidens in the guise of sopranos.

LOCAL GIRL WONDERING
IF THE VIKINGS' INTENTIONS
ARE HONEST

The Middle Ages

So the long night of the Middle Ages descended over Europe. It was every man for himself. On the hilltops and at strong points castles sprang up, and sheltering under them the huts of the peasants.

Society was divided into three classes : lords, serfs, and singers. Women were kept at home, their main purposes being to weave tapestries and to provide inspiration for the wandering minstrels.

The Roman roads had been destroyed during the invasions ; and in winter the countryside was impassable, save by the occasional pilgrim in search of a night's shelter and a game of chess. In short, we can say that for most of the year there was little for these people to do except wait for the excitements of the spring. . . .

"YOUR MOVE, FRIEND!"

"NOT THE SPRING!"

From time immemorial people have done things that at first sight appear so unlikely as to be inexplicable. Thanks to the historian a motive has often been discovered where none seemed possible.

Jousting is a case in point. Medieval artists have portrayed tournaments as a fight between knights. The truth is that the knight, encased in a mass of metal and tapestry and unbalanced by his heavy lance, had difficulty enough in retaining his own seat—let alone unhorsing his opponent. It was for this reason that fences were put up to make the horses run into each other.

The comparative historian, drawing upon Freud and Jung, has little difficulty in relating events in the lists to the mating displays of the animal kingdom.

Years passed in feasting and in fighting ; and where no other opponent offered, there was always the maiden in distress to be rescued from the lurking dragon.

The Medievals were deeply
spiritual, being swayed by religion
rather than reason. It was the era
of the great Gothic cathedrals, of
pilgrimages and prelates, of crusades
to the Holy Land. At one elbow
was God ; at the other the Devil,
always ready to offer a man his
heart's desire in exchange for the
pledge of his soul.

No people were more absorbed
in sombre mysticism than the
Spanish of this period. Engrossed
as they were in a centuries' long
fight against the Moors, they could
not afford with the rest of Europe
to indulge in dragon-killing,
knight errantry, or minstrelsy. As
is evident in our reproduction from
El Greco, this permanently stamped
the national character of Spain.

The Renaissance

Came the dawn of the Renaissance. To the dismay of the clerics, humanists began excavating the bright pagan gods and restoring the broken columns. A vogue was set for archaeology, which has never been altogether lost. Artificial ruins later became a necessity for landscape gardening ; and to the Italians of those days we may trace the American tycoon's instinct to transport castles piecemeal to the Middle West. If the Renaissance started as a nostalgia for the glories of the past, it soon resulted in an eagerness for knowledge. Men looked outwards to the sun and the planets and inwards at the human body, until now a forbidden mystery. With the invention of printing came the discovery that if you repeat something often enough people will end up by believing it.

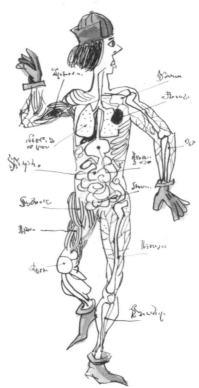

YEARS BEFORE LEASE LEND

The Discovery of America

Map-making was practised long before Columbus, but cartography was then a decorative rather than a practical art. His belief that he could sail round the world met with general ridicule ; and it was rather with the hope of obtaining gold from the fabled lands of India, than of contributing to geography, that the Spanish Court financed his first historic voyage.

Gold there was in America—though not on the scale of the present deposits at Fort Knox. In their search for it, the pale-skinned Conquistadores were received as prophetic descendants of the sun by the astonished Indians, whom they promptly set about massacring and enslaving. The Spaniards were not to exploit the New World in peace. A daring English privateer, Sir Francis Drake, looted their galleons to the tune of half-a-million pounds and provoked the Spanish King to despatch the ill-fated Armada.

THE DISCOVERY OF TOBACCO

The Elizabethan Age

Elizabeth I initiated a golden age in English History. On her accession the country was divided, bankrupt, and at war. Her reign saw lasting religious settlement, economic prosperity, and a resounding naval triumph.

Though she could be cunning, ruthless, and cruel—as witnessed by the execution of Mary Queen of Scots, Essex, and sundry others—it is not for this that Good Queen Bess is remembered. She displayed resolution and acuity of mind that would have been exceptional in a man, and were unheard of in a woman of her period. Her best epitaph is contained in her last address to Parliament : ' This I count the chief glory of my crown, that I have reigned with your loves . . .'

This was the age of Marlowe, of Ben Jonson, of Shakespeare and the Globe Theatre. At one time it was fashionable to attribute Shakespeare's plays to Francis Bacon and others. It was a popular detective game ; but Dr. Johnson's is a truer judgment : ' The stream of time, which is continually washing the dissoluble fabrick of other poets, passes without injury by the adamant of Shakespeare.'

The Seventeenth Century

Our reproduction of Rembrandt's *Anatomy Lesson* exemplifies two outstanding events of the Seventeenth Century : the flowering of the Dutch School of painting and the progress of science.

A falling apple inspired Isaac Newton to one of the greatest feats of the human intelligence, the Law of Universal Gravitation. We may note that his Laws of Motion have far-reaching validity outside the mechanical sphere in which they were strictly intended.

The First Law, which states that every body continues in its state of rest except in so far as it may be compelled by impressed force to change that state, applies generally to legislative bodies when faced with colonial questions and demands for social reform. We shall learn more about this in our chapters on the Colonization of North America and the French Revolution.

Spain stood proudly aloof from the intellectual ferment ; and her hostility illustrates
Newton's Third Law, that action and
reaction are equal and opposite. While
Don Quixote looked resolutely backwards,
his compatriots at the Inquisition interested
themselves solely in the art of roasting.

"It's incredible, he says he never heard of America!"

The New World

The first Englishmen to arrive in North America met with scarcely-clad, but generously-feathered Indians, who believed themselves owners of the land, simply because it had been handed down to them by their forefathers—an erroneous impression speedily to be corrected by the subjects of His Britannic Majesty.

NEW YORKERS OF THE 18TH CENTURY MURMURING AGAINST ENGLAND IN THE SQUARE

The settlers next dealt with the Dutch, Swedes, French, and other interlopers, and finally quarrelled with their own government at home. Many had left England in search of freedom, religious and otherwise, and not unnaturally resented the taxes levied to support an army they considered they neither wanted nor required.

The differences grew ; and when the English tried to tax tea, the colonists retaliated by dumping it into the sea. The Boston Tea Party thus paved the way for the triumph of Coca-Cola. Resolved on ' government of the people, for the people, by the people ', as was declared on a later occasion, the Americans won the War of Independence—and with it all subsequent wars in which they took part.

The Age of Reason

Perhaps in no country is the Eighteenth Century better epitomized than in France. The French are an elegant people ; and it was an age of elegance.

However extreme his views, it was essential for the savant of the period to be suitably attired in cutaway coat, knee breeches, silk stockings, and powdered wig. His culinary requirements were no less demanding ; and in passing, we may remark how fertile of advanced ideas are a good dinner and a glass of Bordeaux.

Be that as it may, Eighteenth-century France confronts us with a galaxy of intellectual talent : in philosophy, Voltaire, Rousseau, and the Encyclopaedists ; in painting, Watteau, Fragonard, and Chardin ; in science, Lamarck, Buffon, and Lavoisier, the father of modern chemistry. Amidst such elevation of the human mind, it is necessary to sound a note of warning. Ever since Descartes thought, and therefore existed, a great many humbler folk had begun to realize that they too existed and would like to share the benefits of universal enlightenment and brotherhood.

PEOPLE OF HIGH STATION
TALKING OF THE RIGHTS
OF MAN

NOBLE RENOUNCING THE BENEFITS
OF UNIVERSAL BROTHERHOOD

The French Revolution

We may state that the French carried elegance too far. Their kings had so far occupied themselves with initiating styles of furniture and installing their mistresses in suitably decorated pavilions, as to be, with few exceptions, completely oblivious of the climate of popular opinion.

Putting the theories of the intelligentsia to a test their authors can hardly have foreseen, the common people asserted their natural rights by slaughtering Louis XVI's soldiers, sacking his palace, and finally decapitating him. There followed a reign of terror, in which the aristocrats were brought to the guillotine by the tumbrilful, to the delight of the *sans culottes*, who thus saw elegance finally extinguished.

It was a blood-bath that served little purpose except to allow the emergence of the Scarlet Pimpernel, who, with Robin Hood and William Tell, was the founder of Television Drama.

The Revolutionaries were no less intransigent abroad than at home, and soon found themselves at war with the rest of Europe. Their leader, Napoleon Bonaparte, starting with the ideals of *Liberté, Egalité, Fraternité*, silenced criticism of these on the home front with a judicious ' whiff of grapeshot ' and subsequently transformed himself into the most cold-blooded conqueror the world had known.

THE IRON HORSE

The Industrial Revolution

In their tight little island across the Channel the English, having disposed of Napoleon on the playing fields of Eton, busied themselves about a different sort of revolution. This stage of history was dominated by the spinning jenny, the mule, and the water frame, appliances mentioned by all serious historians, whose interest in textiles is otherwise confined to Sir Walter Raleigh and the Bayeux tapestry.

These inventions, together with the steam engine, enabled industry to dispense with the master craftsman and to congregate the workers into factories. Hand in hand with technical progress came the discovery that, to quote: 'in the lower orders the deterioration of morals increases with the quantity of unemployed time'. Women and children were therefore drafted from the villages into the coalmines, and the countryside left free for fox-hunting.

THE SHAPE OF
THINGS
TO COME ?

INVENTOR
IN THE AGE OF STEAM

The Romantics

The poor were too busy working the newly-invented machines to reflect that quality had finally been ousted in favour of quantity. This was left to those whom they supported by their labours ; and the well-to-do abandoned themselves to a flood of sentiment.

Goethe, Heine, de Musset, Victor Hugo, and Delacroix were the spearhead of a movement that took emotional intensity for its watchword. Keats, reacting from the products of Birmingham, wrote an Ode on a Grecian Urn. Byron and Shelley rallied to the oppressed Greeks and Italians, it being axiomatic that any people endowed with olive groves, lemon trees, and a rocky coastline stood more in need of help than one's own.

LOVE AT
FIRST SIGHT

THE FIRST BURN IN THE CARPET

The March of Progress

Nineteenth-century progress was so many-sided as to present a host of new problems, both in the drawing-room and further afield.

Whereas our earlier ancestors had led an energetic, outdoor existence, life was now sedentary and safe. It became necessary to go further afield in search of danger and excitement. Since Victorian morality precluded pleasure for its own sake, such expeditions were undertaken on scientific or religious grounds—as, for example, the mapping of remote mountain areas, the provision of hymn books for cannibals, or the decent clothing of the naked and unashamed inhabitants of Darkest Africa.

Fin de Siècle

In Paris the *Fin de Siècle* was greeted by a flurry of artistic activity. The Impressionists and their successors met with a storm of criticism which might well have dismayed the sensitive creators of an earlier age.

'Is not clothedness a distinct type and feature of our Christian faith?' asks a Royal Academician of the period in virtuous indignation. The reaction of the ordinary man to the daring new trends in female attire may be imagined. . . .

It was the quick-witted Parisian café proprietors who first grasped that there are circumstances in which a fully-clothed woman can be as provocative as a nude. Gay Paree was born amidst a flutter of petticoats and silk ; and the can-can, with perfect propriety, travelled West.

"SIR, THE GREAT WAR!"

The First World War

The 1914 war burst upon a world that was not ready for it, preoccupied as the best people were with perfecting the fox-trot and the tango. It began with *éclat* as a war to save civilization, but its tangible results were to perfect the means of mass slaughter and to usher in an era during which queues and shortages became a commonplace.

THE EMERGENCE OF A CLASSLESS SOCIETY

The Western Allies beat Germany on the battlefield, but they certainly lost the peace that followed. In review, the most significant outcome of the 1914 war was the Bolshevik Revolution. Russia steadily grew in importance and created a classless society by the simple expedient of despatching objectors to the salt mines.

The Twenties

In the 1920's people set about making a World Fit For Heroes To Live In. The most important thing was to eradicate any vestige of the preceding epoch. Women in particular had taken advantage of their husbands' absence in the trenches to effect a series of striking reforms. Skirts leapt overnight from the ankles to the knees.

It may be said that women were the only people to win the war, for they now obtained all that the Suffragettes had so noisily demanded, and set out to prove that anything men could do, they could do better.

WOMAN DISCOVERS TOBACCO

Female emancipation reached its ultimate end with a general indulgence in cigarette smoking and cosmetics. Until now lipstick, eye-shadow, and mascara had been the prerogative of the actress and the prostitute.

THE FASHION FOR CUSHIONS
— He seems to be charming, although a little old-fashioned.

The house of the 1920's was swept bare of all the cloying Victorian bric-à-brac now displayed in fashionable antique shops.   Such furniture as remained was inspired by the operating theatre.   The advanced set sat Japanese-style on the floor.

For music the Twenties and Thirties turned to the American negro. Originating in New Orleans, Jazz travelled the Mississippi to Chicago and thereafter swept the United States and the world. Never has any style so divided music lovers. While some found it cacophonous, sour in tone, and out of tune, others were carried away by the frenetic energy of its performers, riding the successive waves of rag-time, the ' blues ', swing, bebop, progressive jazz, and rock-'n-roll. Foremost among its exponents, Louis Armstrong blew all other trumpeters into oblivion.

THE DETECTIVE NOVEL

In literature the Detective Novel soon outstripped all other forms. Its subject was an ingeniously contrived murder, preferably of an Englishman and taking place at a house party crammed with suspect and unlikely characters. The subsequent problem has not been to write novels, plays, or scripts, but to find a reader without an unpublished manuscript of his own.

AT LAST! A READER!

The Dictators

In Germany, a house-painter called Adolf Schickelgruber had so little success in his trade that he changed his name to Hitler and rallied the populace to the menace of Communism. In this he was supported by Mussolini in Italy, but bitterly opposed by the Russian dictator, Stalin, who inveighed against the Capitalists.

—These are surprising results for tanks made of cardboard.

To begin with both Mussolini and Hitler were regarded with some sympathy in the Democracies as strong men who had rescued their countries from post-war decline. Nazi Germany was allowed a token army; and visitors commented on her surprisingly realistic 'cardboard' tanks. It was generally agreed that Mussolini was the saviour of the Italian railway system.

WONDERFUL MUSSOLINI! THE TRAINS ARRIVE ON TIME.

LEAGUE OF NATIONS
" We all know that war is
a thing of the past

GENTLEMEN OF THE SEVENTEENTH CENTURY FORSWEARING WAR

The prime aim of the 1920's and 1930's was to abolish war ; and for this purpose the League of Nations was instituted. To the pained surprise of the politicians, Hitler and Mussolini began ignoring its most solemn decisions. Hitler, having decimated the Jews at home, turned his attentions abroad ; and Mussolini loosed his fury on tiny Abyssinia. What particularly riled the professional statesmen was that each fresh *coup* took place at weekends sacrosanct to fishing and shooting of a different kind. A new World War was on its way. . . .

PEACE AT LAST — 1945

The Present Day

To the best of our ability we have led the reader through the mists of legend and miracle. It may be that we have blundered in the dark night of the Middle Ages or come nigh to foundering among the troubled waters of the Renaissance. For the historian, the hard ground of fact too often turns out to be a quagmire of opinion and prejudice.

We have done our best; and having set foot on the shores of the present, let us examine them in the light of the past. Has not a justly famous colleague defined the purpose of history as ' to tell what man is by telling him what man has done ' ? This we now propose to do; and our method will be comparative. . . .

1800
HIGH
WAIST-
LINE

1885
WAIST-LINE
INDEFINITE

Evolution in dress—that is to
say, women's dress—largely
resolves itself into an attempt to
establish a waistline. Should
this be at the neck, the knees,
or where?

WOMAN'S EFFORTS TO ESTABLISH A WAISTLINE

After centuries of experiment
there seemed general agreement
in 1955 that the best place for the
waistline was the waist. This
was to reckon without the Paris
dress houses, whose decrees
women disregard if they Dior.

1925
LOW
WAIST-
LINE

1955
WAIST-LINE
AT THE
WAIST

Ours is the era of the machine, of the second
generation machine, automated, remotely-controlled,
springing into action at the behest of an electronic brain.
No longer is Man a slave to his environment.   The
Wonders of the Ancient World pale in comparison
with such projects as the harnessing of the atom.   The
mere touch of a button suffices to set in motion the
untapped resources of Nature. . . .

Perhaps nowhere have the advances been more spectacular than in the field of transport. It is true that the jet engine was pioneered by the Arabians; but they cannot have foreseen a period when it would become quicker for the businessman to travel from London to Paris than from his office, home. It is sober fact that by the Seventies it will be possible to board a supersonic aircraft at lunchtime and to cross the Atlantic to New York in time for breakfast the same morning.

THE FIRST QUEUE

Many motorists, baffled by the congestion on the roads, prefer to leave their cars permanently in the garage during the working year, and to ship them by rail or air to beat the holiday traffic jams. In the field of public transport, too, certain basic difficulties have still to be overcome.

The speeding of transport, the growth of mechanization, the perfecting of mass production, all tend towards the same end. It is all very well to introduce a forty-hour week, or a forty-minute week—if work *has* to be rationed. Short of raising the school leaving age to thirty-five—and it must be admitted that large sections of the population have no scholastic bent—the gaping problem that faces modern man is what to do with the time that is saved.

    Above : A group of cavemen tackle the problem of leisure.

    Below : A Twentieth-century solution.

Above and on the following pages we further examine the problem of how to kill time—if you have no better use for it.

Sport as we know it has developed from the ancient pastimes of the chase and the joust. Nowhere is this better seen than in the bullring, where man still pits the quickness of foot and eye against an animal—albeit a smaller animal—with nothing to help him but an armed picador on a padded horse, another three assistants with darts, and a stout wooden barrier.

THERE WAS ONCE NO KUDOS IN KILLING A <u>BULL</u>

PREHISTORIC COMBAT

Single-handed combat is still popular ; but in modern sport the emphasis has shifted from the participants to the spectators and promoters.

Vast crowds assemble, and enormous sums of money change hands in the form of gate money and bets. And sport is political dynamite, now that the loss of a football match can cause a diplomatic incident.

MODERN ALL-IN WRESTLING

LIBRARY & MUSEUM

FOOTBALL CROWD

As we have seen, the origins of the theatre were religious. In an increasingly materialistic age, when the theatre itself has given way to the cinema and television, Man has created for himself a new pantheon—of 'stars', whether of sport, the stage, or the screen.

The early film stars, like Chaplin and Garbo, were performers of outstanding talent; but Time Marches On, and if man is to make gods in his own image, it is clearly democratic and desirable for all stars to be as alike and indistinguishable as beauty queens.

Like the temple which preceded it, the modern movie house is a dimly-lit edifice
of vast size. Movie idols resemble their predecessors in size and scale, but are no
longer made of wood or stone, nor are they completely static. They materialize
on all-developing, curved screens, their features occasionally coming to life in a
ten-foot smile. Modern developments in Smell-o-VisioN make it possible for
the auditorium to be impregnated, not with myrrh or incense, but with the more
exotic perfumes of cigar smoke or suntan lotion.

"WOULD YOU MIND DECLARING INDEPENDENCE A LITTLE FURTHER AWAY?"

THE IRON CURTAIN

In world politics there have been two major developments since the Second World War.

The first is the desire of the smaller countries in Africa and the East to break away from their colonial status and declare themselves independent. Depending on one's viewpoint, this is either a chauvinistic lapse into anarchy and Communism ; or alternatively a praiseworthy attempt to escape from Imperialistic domination. In the Middle East, the presence of oil adds fuel to the flames.

The other great trend is the division of the world into two massive blocs : on one side of the Iron Curtain the United States and her allies, on the other the Communist countries in sway of Soviet Russia. Both have one thing in common—a determination to be better armed than the other fellow.

"But nobody has anything to fear from us !"

The scientist occupies a central position in modern society. In Victorian times he was the precursor of an age of plenty ; in the popular imagination he is nowadays a sinister figure behind the scenes, a tool in the power of either the Capitalists or the Soviets.

The public is hardly to blame in this view. So deluged have they been by newspaper articles about the fearful effects of the atomic bomb that it is little wonder if, like their forebears, people look into the skies and read the portents of disaster.

More tangible than Flying Saucers are the measurable effects of atomic experiment—for war and peace alike—in the shape of fall-out from explosions, contaminated pastures, radioactive dumps, the increase in cancer of the blood. . . .

The escapist's last refuge used to be a South Sea island. Now the South Seas are a semi-permanent 'prohibited area'.

"TELL ME IF ANYTHING INTERESTING HAPPENS"

"WHAT I LIKE ABOUT PEACE IS THE CHANCE
TO DEVOTE ONESELF TO FRUITFUL RESEARCH"

The pace quickens. With science and technology making giant strides, the space-ships and the rockets no longer belong to science fiction. Man has reached the moon, and his rockets are probing into outer space. The earth is too small to contain him ; and the astronauts are preparing for a voyage without foreseeable end.

We, as sober historians, do not attempt to predict the shape of things to come. We would not even wish to bury the old Adam, were that a possibility— are not the space-ships of today a fruit of his inquisitiveness ? Rather we hope that, if history is largely a chapter of mistakes, the new Conquistador, on his way to Venus or beyond, may ponder and profit by his earthy origins.

He his fabric of the Heavens
Hath left to their disputes, perhaps to move
His laughter at their quaint opinions wide
Hereafter, when they come to model Heaven
And calculate the stars, how they will wield
The mighty frame, how build, unbuild, contrive
To save appearances, how gird the sphere
With centric and eccentric scribbled o'er
Cycle and epicycle, orb in orb.

Milton, *Paradise Lost*, VIII, 76–84

PITHECANTHRUPUS ERECTUS

HOMO SAPIENS